LET'S COOK WITH
Popcorn!

Delicious & Fun Popcorn Dishes Kids Can Make

Nancy Tuminelly

Consulting Editor, Diane Craig, M.A./Reading Specialist

A Division of ABDO

ABDO
Publishing Company

visit us at www.abdopublishing.com

Published by ABDO Publishing Company, a division of ABDO, P.O. Box 398166, Minneapolis, Minnesota 55439.
Copyright © 2013 by Abdo Consulting Group, Inc. International copyrights reserved in all countries. No part of this book may be reproduced in any form without written permission from the publisher. Super SandCastle™ is a trademark and logo of ABDO Publishing Company.

Printed in the United States of America, North Mankato, Minnesota
062012
092012

 PRINTED ON RECYCLED PAPER

Editor: Liz Salzmann
Content Developer: Nancy Tuminelly
Cover and Interior Design and Production: Colleen Dolphin, Mighty Media, Inc.
Food Production: Desirée Bussiere
Photo Credits: Colleen Dolphin, Shutterstock, iStockphoto (Gary Milner, Dawna Stafford)

The following manufacturers/names appearing in this book are trademarks: Brer Rabbit® Molasses, Calumet® Baking Powder, Gold Medal® All-Purpose Flour, Karo® Light Corn Syrup, Market Pantry® Pure Vanilla Extract, Nestlé NESQUIK® Chocolate Powder, PAM® Baking Spray, Pyrex® Measuring Glass, Quaker® Yellow Corn Meal, Roundy's® Distilled White Vinegar, Roundy's® No-Stick Butter Cooking Spray

Library of Congress Cataloging-in-Publication Data
Tuminelly, Nancy, 1952-
Let's cook with popcorn! : delicious & fun popcorn dishes kids can make / Nancy Tuminelly.
    p. cm. -- (Super simple recipes)
  ISBN 978-1-61783-423-3
  1. Cooking (Popcorn)--Juvenile literature. 2. Snack foods--Juvenile literature. I. Title.
  TX814.5.P66T86 2012
  641.6'5677--dc23
                          2011052197

Super SandCastle™ books are created by a team of professional educators, reading specialists, and content developers around five essential components—phonemic awareness, phonics, vocabulary, text comprehension, and fluency—to assist young readers as they develop reading skills and strategies and increase their general knowledge. All books are written, reviewed, and leveled for guided reading, early reading intervention, and Accelerated Reader® programs for use in shared, guided, and independent reading and writing activities to support a balanced approach to literacy instruction.

Note to Adult Helpers

Helping kids learn how to cook is fun! It's a great way to practice math and science. Cooking teaches kids about responsibility and boosts their confidence. Plus, they learn how to help out in the kitchen! The recipes in this book require adult assistance. Make sure there is always an adult around when kids are in the kitchen. Expect kids to make a mess, but also expect them to clean up after themselves. Most importantly, make the experience pleasurable by sharing and enjoying the food kids make.

Symbols

Knife
Always ask an adult to help you use knives.

Microwave
Be careful with hot food! Learn more on page 7.

Oven
Have an adult help put things into and take them out of the oven. Learn more on page 7.

Stovetop
Be careful around hot burners! Learn more on page 7.

Nuts
Some people can get very sick if they eat nuts.

Contents

Let's Cook with Popcorn!

Popcorn is native to North America. People have been eating it for thousands of years. Popcorn has also been used in **ceremonies** and for decoration.

Popcorn is a favorite snack for many people. Americans eat about 17 **billion** quarts of popcorn every year! It is a healthy food, if you don't add a lot of butter, salt, or sugar. And it is delicious and easy to make. See page 11.

The recipes in this book are simple. It's fun using one main ingredient! Cooking teaches you about food, measuring, and following directions. Enjoy your tasty treats with your family and friends!

Think Safety!

- Ask an adult to help you use knives. Use a cutting board.

- Clean up spills to prevent accidents.

- Keep tools and **utensils** away from the edge of the table or counter.

- Use a step stool if you cannot reach something.

- Tie back long hair or wear a hat.

- Don't wear loose clothes. Roll up long **sleeves**.

- Keep a fire extinguisher in the cooking area.

Cooking Basics

Before you start...

- Get **permission** from an adult.
- Wash your hands.
- Read the recipe at least once.
- Set out all the ingredients and tools you will need.

When you're done...

- Cover food with plastic wrap or aluminum foil. Use **containers** with lids if you have them.
- Wash all of the dishes and **utensils**.
- Put all of the ingredients and tools back where you found them.
- Clean up your work space.

Using the Microwave

- Use microwave-safe dishes.

- Never put aluminum foil or metal in the microwave.

- Start with a short cook time. If it's not enough, cook it some more.

- Use oven mitts when taking things out of the microwave.

- Stop the microwave to stir liquids during heating.

Using the Stovetop

- Turn pot handles away from the burners and the edge of the stove.

- Use the temperature setting in the recipe.

- Use pot holders to handle hot pots and pans.

- Do not leave metal **utensils** in pots.

- Don't put anything except pots and pans on or near the burners.

- Use a timer. Check the food and cook it more if needed.

Using the Oven

- Use the temperature setting in the recipe.

- Preheat the oven while making the recipe.

- Use oven-safe dishes.

- Use pot holders or oven mitts to handle baking sheets and dishes.

- Do not touch oven doors. They can be very hot.

- Set a timer. Check the food and bake it more if needed.

A microwave, stovetop, and oven are very useful for cooking food. But they can be **dangerous** if you are not careful. Always ask an adult for help.

Measuring

Wet Ingredients

Set a measuring cup on the counter.
Add the liquid until it reaches
the amount you need. Check the
measurement from eye level.

Dry Ingredients

Use a spoon to put the dry
ingredient in the measuring cup or
spoon. Put more than you need in
the measuring cup or spoon. Run
the back of a dinner knife across
the top. This removes the extra.

Moist Ingredients

Moist ingredients are things
such as brown sugar and dried
fruit. They need to be packed
down into the measuring cup.
Keep packing until the ingredient
reaches the measurement line.

Do You Know This = That?

There are different ways to measure the same amount.

 =

3 teaspoons = 1 tablespoon   4 tablespoons = ¼ cup   5 tablespoons + 1 teaspoon = ⅓ cup

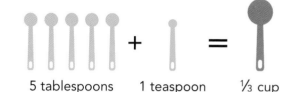

 =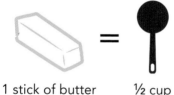

16 tablespoons = 1 cup   1 cup = 8 ounces   1 stick of butter = ½ cup

   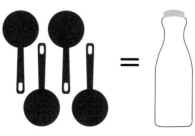   

2 cups = 1 pint   4 cups = 1 quart   2 quarts = ½ gallon

Cooking Terms

Mix
Combine ingredients with a mixing spoon. *Stir* is another word for mix.

Grease
Cover something with butter, oil, or cooking spray.

Chop
Cut something into very small pieces with a knife.

Fry
Cook in hot oil or butter until a brown crust forms.

Coat
Stir or shake something in an ingredient until it is covered.

Boil
Heat liquid until it begins to bubble.

Spread
Make a smooth layer with a spoon, knife, or spatula.

Crush
Mash food into **crumbs** or small pieces.

Making Popcorn

Freshly popped popcorn is always the best! You can use an air popper or buy packages of microwave popcorn. Here are two other ways to make popcorn.

Stovetop Popcorn

1. Put 3 tablespoons of vegetable oil in a medium pot. Put the lid on the pot. Heat it over medium-high heat.

2. Cover the bottom of the pot with one layer of popcorn kernels. Put the lid on the pot.

3. Wait for the popcorn to start popping. Then gently move the pot back and forth. Do not shake it! When the popping slows down, open the lid slightly. This lets the steam out.

4. Wait until the popping slows to every 2 to 3 seconds. Pour the popcorn into a bowl. Toss with salt.

Homemade Microwave Popcorn

1. Put ¼ cup of popcorn in a lunch-size paper bag. Fold the top over several times.

2. Microwave on high for 2 minutes. If it is still popping, microwave it for 30 more seconds. Keep adding time until it only pops once every few seconds.

3. Be careful opening the bag! It will be steaming hot! Pour the popcorn into a bowl. Toss with salt.

Tools

mixing spoon

liquid measuring cup

paper grocery bag

9 x 13-inch
baking sheet

cutting board

oven mitts

pot holders

serving bowl

dry measuring cups

measuring spoons

rolling pin

parchment paper

fork

whisk

sharp knife

candy thermometer

timer

spoon

wax paper

container with lid

plastic zipper bags

muffin tin

mixing bowls

medium pot

large pot

Ingredients

carob pieces

dried fruit

molasses

sweetened
condensed milk

non-stick
cooking spray

eggs

Dijon mustard

butter

baking powder

vanilla extract

butter-flavored
cooking spray

butter-flavored salt

cornmeal

all-purpose flour

salt

light corn syrup

popcorn, popped

white vinegar

maple syrup

powdered
hot cocoa mix

popcorn kernels

bacon

sugar

brown sugar

milk

pumpkin seeds

peanuts

chili powder

ground cumin

Spanish peanuts

soy nuts

ground cinnamon

ground nutmeg

Oh-So-Good Popcorn Mix

A healthy snack everyone will love!

Makes 6 servings

ingredients

8 cups popcorn, popped
butter-flavored salt
½ cup peanuts
1 cup dried fruit
½ cup soy nuts
½ cup pumpkin seeds
¾ cup carob pieces

tools

large plastic zipper bag
measuring cups
mixing bowl
mixing spoon
serving bowls

1. Put the popcorn in a large plastic zipper bag. Sprinkle with butter-flavored salt. Close the bag. Shake well.

2. Mix the rest of the ingredients in a bowl. Add them to the bag.

3. Close the bag. Shake it to mix the ingredients. Now it's ready to eat!

TIP: If a nut **allergy** is a concern, use more of another ingredient instead of the peanuts.

Maple Bacon Kettle Corn

A sweet and salty delight that melts in your mouth!

Makes 8 servings

ingredients

4 slices bacon, fried and
    chopped
1 tablespoon maple syrup
¼ cup bacon grease, saved
    after frying the bacon
½ cup popcorn kernels
3 tablespoon sugar
1½ teaspoon salt

tools

knife
cutting board
measuring cups
measuring spoons
small mixing bowl
mixing spoon
large pot
pot holders

1. Mix bacon pieces and maple syrup in a small bowl.

2. Put the bacon grease in a large pot. If you don't have enough grease, add canola oil to make ¼ cup. Add the popcorn kernels. Sprinkle with the sugar and 1 teaspoon salt.

3. Cover the pot. Heat over medium heat.

4. Wait for the popcorn to start popping. Every 1 to 2 minutes, move the pot gently back and forth. Use pot holders to hold the lid on.

5. When it's done popping, remove the pot from the heat. Add ½ teaspoon salt and the bacon mixture. Mix well.

Mexican Popcorn Olé

A delicious way to spice up popcorn!

Makes 10 servings

ingredients

12 cups popcorn, popped
2 tablespoons butter, melted
1 tablespoon Dijon mustard
2 teaspoons chili powder
¼ teaspoon salt
¼ teaspoon ground cumin

tools

mixing bowls
measuring cups
measuring spoons
spoon
mixing spoon
container with lid

1 Put the popcorn in a large bowl.

2 Put the rest of the ingredients in a small bowl. Mix well.

3 Pour the wet mixture over the popcorn. Mix well.

4 Store in a **container** with a lid.

Cocoa-latta Popcorn

A sweet and tasty dessert snack!

Makes 12 to 16 servings

ingredients

16 cups popcorn, popped

butter-flavored cooking spray,
 chilled

12 tablespoons powdered
 hot cocoa mix

4 tablespoons
 ground cinnamon

tools

paper grocery bag

measuring cups

measuring spoons

small mixing bowl

mixing spoon

serving bowls

1 Pour 4 cups of popcorn into the grocery bag. Spray lightly with cooking spray. Close the bag. Shake to coat popcorn.

2 Repeat step 1 until all of the popcorn is in the bag.

3 Put the cocoa mix and cinnamon in a small bowl. Mix well.

4 Put one-quarter of the cocoa mixture into the grocery bag. Shake well to coat popcorn.

5 Repeat step 4 until all of the cocoa mixture is in the bag.

6 Put the coated popcorn in serving bowls. Eat up!

Nutty Caramel Popcorn

Better than store-bought and easy to make!

Makes 8 servings

ingredients

16 cups popcorn, popped
1 cup Spanish peanuts
4 tablespoons butter
1 cup brown sugar
½ cup light corn syrup
⅛ cup molasses
¼ teaspoon salt

tools

large mixing bowl
mixing spoon
medium pot
measuring cups
measuring spoons
9 × 13-inch baking sheet
parchment paper
oven mitts
timer

1 Preheat the oven to 300 **degrees**. Mix the popcorn and peanuts in the large mixing bowl. Set aside.

2 Put the rest of the ingredients in a pot. Bring to a boil over medium-high heat. Stir often. Boil for 20 to 25 minutes. Remove from heat when the mixture begins to turn dark brown.

3 Pour the warm mixture over the popcorn mixture. Stir to coat the popcorn evenly.

4 Cover the baking sheet with parchment paper. Spread the popcorn mixture over it. Bake for 15 minutes. Stir every 5 minutes.

5 Remove from oven. Cool for 15 to 20 minutes.

Poppin' Popcorn Balls

A sweet ball of fun for every party!

Makes 6 servings

ingredients

2 cups sugar

½ cup light corn syrup

1 teaspoon white vinegar

½ teaspoon salt

1 teaspoon vanilla extract

18 cups popcorn, popped

tools

medium pot

measuring cups

measuring spoons

mixing spoon

candy thermometer

large mixing bowl

wax paper

timer

1 Put the sugar, corn syrup, vinegar, salt, and 1⅓ cups water in a medium pot. Stir.

2 Bring to a boil over high heat. Put the candy thermometer in the pot. Boil the mixture until it reaches 255 **degrees**. Remove from heat. Stir in the vanilla.

3 Put the popcorn in a large bowl. Pour the sugar mixture over the popcorn. Stir gently to coat the popcorn.

4 Let the popcorn cool for 5 to 10 minutes. Lightly grease your hands. Press the popcorn into 3-inch balls.

5 Set the balls on wax paper to cool.

Pop-corny Cookies

Yummy treats for lunch or snack time!

Makes 12 cookies

ingredients

1 cup all-purpose flour

4 teaspoons baking powder

1½ teaspoons ground nutmeg

1 cup cornmeal

1 teaspoon salt

1 cup sugar

½ cup butter, melted

1 egg, beaten

¼ cup sweetened
   condensed milk

1 cup popcorn, crushed

1 cup dried fruit; chopped

tools

knife

cutting board

measuring
cups & spoons

fork or whisk

mixing spoon

mixing bowls

9 × 13-inch
baking sheet

oven mitts

timer

1 Preheat the oven to 425 **degrees**. Put the flour, baking powder, nutmeg, cornmeal, and salt in a medium bowl. Stir well.

2 Put the sugar, butter, egg, milk, and ¼ cup water in a large bowl. Stir well.

3 Slowly stir the dry mixture into the wet mixture. Add the popcorn and dried fruit. Mix well.

4 Grease the baking sheet. Use a ½ tablespoon to drop the cookies onto the baking sheet. Bake for 10 to 12 minutes.

TIP: To crush popcorn, put it in a large plastic zipper bag. Roll over it with a rolling pin.

Popcorn Muffin Delights

Scrumptious for breakfast or any time!

Makes 6 muffins

ingredients

1½ cups all-purpose flour

3 teaspoons baking powder

1 teaspoon salt

1 tablespoon sugar

1 cup milk

¾ cup popcorn, popped

1 egg, beaten

2 tablespoons butter, melted

non-stick cooking spray

tools

large plastic
zipper bag

rolling pin

mixing bowl

fork or whisk

measuring
cups & spoons

mixing spoon

muffin tin

spoon

oven mitts

timer

1   Preheat the oven to 425 **degrees**.

2   Put the popcorn in a large plastic zipper bag. Roll over it with a rolling pin to crush the popcorn.

3   Mix the flour, baking powder, salt, and sugar in a large bowl. Add the milk, popcorn, egg, and butter. Stir well.

4   Lightly spray the muffin tin with cooking spray. Fill the muffin cups two-thirds full.

5   Bake for 25 minutes.

TIP: Serve the muffins with honey or jelly!

Glossary

allergy – sickness caused by touching, breathing, or eating certain things.

billion – a very large number. One billion is also written 1,000,000,000.

ceremony – an important event that often includes special clothes, music, dances, and speeches.

container – something that other things can be put into.

crumb – a tiny piece of something, especially something baked, such as bread or crackers.

dangerous – able or likely to cause harm or injury.

degree – the unit used to measure temperature.

permission – when a person in charge says it's okay to do something.

sleeve – the part of a piece of clothing that covers some or all of the arm.

utensil – a tool used to prepare or eat food.